PROPHET CALLED TO A CROSS CULTURE

Ken Cox

REJOICE
Essential Publishing

Ken Cox/Rejoice Essential Publishing
PO BOX 512
Effingham, SC 29541
www.republishing.org

Unless otherwise indicated, scripture is taken from the King James Version.'

Prophet Called to a Cross Culture/Ken Cox

ISBN-13: 978-1-956775-37-2
LCCN: 2022914341

Table of Contents

INTRODUCTION

My Prophetic friend, let me ask you, what happens when God has called you to the nations and you are sent to people you have little to nothing in common with? You may be like me and realize the opportunity is a sure sign I needed to grow. I was prepared, but I still needed to grow. This is a critical point that I will pound on throughout this book. I pray this work will alert you to a need to know your culture before becoming a self-appointed prophetic expert on someone else's culture.

Remembering clearly, in my first assignment to the nations, the cross-culture factor for me was only a surface issue. I did not fully understand it or appreciate the moment, much less the even more profound issues of relevance.

I was prepared for a cross-culture assignment as a prophet. I was to complete my assignment. Much of my instruction was on-the-job training. God allowed me to make mistakes, and He still blessed me. I was a prophet with a Jonah mentality, so there was plenty of room for growth.

My view of this surface issue had me excited and nervous at the same time. Have you ever had that feeling upon you? It is an unsteady feeling as you think and focus on what may or may not happen. Stop now and think about it. You will start to see the connection with our cultural views today.

This book will be filled with real-life experiences and real-life reflection. I write this book from a perspective influenced by my culture to the Prophets and the Ekklesia. I'm led to share with you what I have learned as I seek to see how God will allow it to manifest in the next level of His Glory.

I firmly believe in a now day reality with remnants of change. The remnants only seem to be temporary at best compared to the reality of our lives.

Do not misunderstand me; my faith in God is not what I will question. The experience of this book will challenge you as a prophet on the issues of our cultures.

Let me warn you; you may read teachings that may not line up with some cultural customs and traditions on several uncomfortable topics. My mantel has me focused on reaching my assigned destiny, just like anyone else. I am assigned to work with multiple cultures as a prophet called to nations, and I am still learning much of and from them.

This is why I ask you to read and understand that this is not for everyone, but this is the remnant that will work with me and others as we stop talking about change and we actually realize we are the assigned ones of the promised manifestation. We must bring the Ekklesia together, not just with our talk but our actions.

Maybe your soul can witness as mine does, as we reflect on what it takes to go into a cross-culture and operate in the anointing that is upon your life. This is an anointing that will be described in many ways, just as the now day Ekklesia itself has been. This is why some readers will have issues with Prophets of a Cross Culture. My assignment is to expand perspectives.

I strive not to pump you up, my prophetic friends and curious readers; we have far too much work to do to understand cross-culture ministry. We have dealt with enough in our lives to know that if we are to be relevant in establishing the Ekklesia, then the issue of understanding cross-cultures is critical. The very essence of a Prophet called to the nations simply starts the preparation process. The Bible itself is a cross-cultural work.

Many of us today simply do not fully understand our original birthed culture. That is an issue all to itself, but we have to examine it to understand the cross-culture. My prophetic friend, as you read this, grab a cup of your favorite tea, juice, or bottled water. Let's talk about some issues. Question? Are you a prophet in a cross-culture?

CHAPTER 1

WHAT IS CULTURE TO ME, THE PROPHET?

Becoming a prophet called to the nations will expose you to a culture different from yours. The Word of God is a work geared to cross cultures. Have you ever wondered why so many of us never learn or understand different cultures? Here is where the work begins for so many of us as prophets.

Let us define culture as an established norm of a group of people. A culture can be customs or traditions that define a way of life. There are cultures of prophetic works that relate to different cultures, nations, and people. This is cross-culture as we strive to understand and develop the importance of the concept. Prophets, with Christ as our center, we should see the influence of the anointing move between two or more cultures.

Here, we start on the delicate, not discussed, under-discussed topics of cross-cultural or intercultural ministry. Prophets, there is also the issue of how we relate to and deal with those who are different. This includes communicating with unfamiliar things like different cultures or nations.

To further complicate the issue, we must be aware of subcultures; they can be an act or an instance of thinking or belief away from an established culture. Each of us as prophets needs to understand that our soul is busy as it maintains our culture. The soul is a constant identifier of your generic culture.

The soul controls and is central to how you as a prophet think about yourself. Your growth as a prophet, knowing who you are and how you feel about yourself shapes your cultural and spiritual identity. This is relevant despite your diverse experiences, economic status, or educational background.

Let us now define a prophetic subculture as a group of prophets with a culture. These prophets can be different from the culture but belong in the culture. We must also note that prophets have a subculture within any prophetic subculture. There also can be a counterculture. An example of this is the same or similar way of thinking or processing information in a certain way.

Moses was part of the Egyptian culture. His mentality was divided between the Hebrew culture and the Egyptian culture. He was divided as he saw a reflection of himself. May I suggest you read my book, "*Meeting The Prophet in My Reflection.*"

I spend time detailing the saga of Moses, torn between understanding his current culture and who he was. The now-generation prophet must understand this before you go to the nations. You must understand the cultural issues before you are sent to work in cross-cultural ministry work, which prepares you for greater.

With that being said, what's the issue? The issue is that there is a difference between the various training standards within the prophetic realm. This difference varies with different standards and norms. The soul is at work with the gathering and connecting us to cultures that we identify with, despite our differences in this process evolving.

While we are in this evolving process of ethnic, regional, and economic issues, it directly affects how we train and who trains us. Let's say who we allow to train us. The reality of becoming a prophetic social group is ever-present. The reality that key factors must be in place is understood.

The social group now seeks to distinguish itself through characteristic patterns and accepted norms. This is a culture within a culture. This culture has things it believes in and things it deems important and critical. The culture's factors will make it think and feel a certain way, especially now in our generation. I will discuss this in chapter two of this book, called *"My Culture And How It Affects Me And Not You."*

Let's now look at this closely and consider the prophets part of the kingdom culture and the fact that the prophetic exhibits, patterns, and characteristics are not found in the core gifting of other gifts in the Body of Christ. This is due to the fact that God created us differently. I am making a point here that will be reflected in the following chapters.

Prophets since our training is often different, and yet we realize that our efforts reflect a futile training on how to bring ourselves together within the Ekklesia. How do we grow it despite our cultural differences?

We look at the same world and issues and see it differently based on our culture. This is a fact, and we speak of our growth in Christ and our relationships, yet our ability to operate cross-culturally seems at best limited and more like scattered remnants of what we can be in God.

Let us not ignore the fact that our social standards have an extreme effect on this. We often, as prophets, feel neglected and do not understand why. This becomes our sense of identity, as we have discussed. The Prophet Jeremiah is a perfect example of this. Imagine how he felt neglected and criticized by his family (Jeremiah 16).

The human laptop, your soul, is the central processing place of your culture and subculture. You're a prophet, and God has sent you to the nations; there are at least five keys I now want to discuss with you as you read this and process your personal prophetic subculture.

Take these 5 points to heart; they will help you understand the opportunity of going to the nations and how you must be prepared. Again, remember I said you're going to the nations, and the bottom line is that it means a different culture from your core culture.

1. Your soul deals with the negative or ambivalent relations with other ministers. There will be other men and women of God who may not understand the prophet or have been hurt by what they consider true

prophetic ministry. You, as the prophet, should be aware of this, and your self-awareness center of the prophet is how you must understand. This is a definite subculture you, as a prophet, will deal with. This will form because of the thinking and processing of the prophets and the men and women of God.

2. Your soul, with your associations and divine connections, will dictate your journey of being sent to the nations. Who are you connected to? Will you listen to God and establish relationships that may be uncommon to you but yet in His will for you? The fact is, that many times, you will be a loaner in your own area. This is a subculture itself simply because you are a loaner. Prophet, you must understand that you are in a group here that is actually a counterculture within the subculture of your prophetic mantle.

3. Your soul must process and maintain your prophetic status despite how your peers may treat you. Yes, this can be in your local area. The human aspect of your soul will manage and navigate through sporadic offerings of belonging as a prophet. Simply allow God to use you. Soon your ability to discern secret unspoken jealousy through your local peers and others in the Body of Christ will become something you learn how to manage.

The prophet is not without honor in his own country. Do you remember when Jesus returned home, and He only healed a few people? The townspeople were jealous and couldn't understand who Jesus really was. You will experience this also in a unique way. The soul will deal with the exaggeration in the minds of haters and those who don't understand. This will include times when you were mistreated and misunderstood. Here you see yourself in yet another type of culturally connected group.

4. The Soul of the Prophet operates through a refusal to adhere to the regularity of ordinary life. The culture of the prophet is built on this principle in relation to what God wants. We are the Prophetic Culture. We are different and we know it.

Amos 3:7 identifies us as the servants of His will as He reveals His plans to us. We are prophets, seers, watchmen, and, yes, apostles. We want more of God. We demand more of God within ourselves and others who come into our lives for seasons or reasons.

Our many multiple prophetic subcultures provide a wide variety that entices and influences the present generation and emerging prophets in many ways. This is an absolute fact. Our world is currently dominated by everything not of God to include, including disrespect, indignity, and even the destruction of the physical body.

The most effective subculture in destroying prophets of this generation is the subculture of nonbelief. My friend, are you aware of this? We do not believe in responsibility or accountability. Our flawed reasoning and failure to discern hindrances kill our ability to live with God fully. Personal blemishes of prophets are truly the culture of this age.

How does a prophet deal with all of these subcultures? The answer is that the principles of the Bible rise higher than any other culture or subculture. When God saves us, we are new creatures.

When you grow and mature, you will see the prophetic changes in your manner of living. Your new-found maturity transports you into a nobility of living and talking with respect—prophets, we are not to be conformed to this world, its culture, and sounds.

Ephesians 5:27 declares, *"Not having a spot, not having or wrinkle, being holy with no blemish."* Prophets, we must understand that no matter what defects of the flesh and life we have, we must come to Christ with them for healing!

5. 2 Corinthians 5 says that we will become new in Him since old things are passed away. Funny how some prophets hate to give up unproductive habits. Who is a member of this prophetic subculture? The truth is, we all are at some point in time. That is a fact, so we must grow up as prophets from the immature, childish things and grow up into Christ! I am convinced that the Ekklesia must have this from the prophet.

Paul says, "As a child, I spoke, but he became a man and put away childish things." The putting away of silly things is in our manner of living. These are the foundations of decisions and choices that determine whether we will trust God.

Notice that when Daniel entered the consecrated life of Romans 12:1, 2. Daniel had already committed himself through meditation on the Word of God and communion with the Lord; these already occupied first place in his life. This is the task and standards we must have in our subculture daily as prophets.

Prophets, these are critical points we must realize about cultures before we go to the nations and establish the Ekklesia. Yes, this is before we are released for cross-culture ministry. We need to understand our culture thoroughly.

We have established that your thought life as a prophet is important as it relates to the heart, not to defile yourself. This is the foundation of the decisive stand with the prophet's faith laying hold on God for strength that will follow. Every prophet who goes through his or her process shall find themselves.

Daniel purposed in his heart not to be defiled by what the world feeds from and refused to be influenced by them as he was able to establish a culture, as he thought and did. We should be the same way. This is a prophet who was not afraid. Yes, similar convictions are imperative in the Ekklesia today.

This is our subculture in the Body of Christ, within the gifts of 5-fold ministry, and within the gifts themselves. This includes a subculture of the prophetic and a subculture or even a counterculture within it.

The prophet learns that faithfulness of the Lord becomes a blessed reality in the path of separation from the world and sin and separation unto God! This is the subculture of the prophet.

Why are we wondering why some people have rejected us? They have seen us as a culture of the wild and rebellious. They have seen us moving in and out of denominations and abandoning our core doctrines altogether. They want some truth and are wrestling with life for just that. As prophets, we should represent that but do we?

Our creation is of a subculture of prophets who seem to have it together, but hidden demons constantly plague us. Prophets so often are on display; we are expected to be among the most genuine examples of being Christ-like. Yes, we know we will not fit the traditional Christian mold.

God will send us to people who need our help. We should be able and anointed to help them, but we are not because we are locked in a subculture of procrastination, laziness, and a refusal to learn.

We call it the prophetic, but how few of us are ready to ascend to the heights God has called us to because of our refusal to walk in the blind faith that God uses to qualify us for His work at the signs, wonders, and miracles level.

Prophets, everything we do should be by God's Word; it is the cross-culture reference we need to study and absorb. The conclusion is that if I'm going to be God's prophet, I needed to discover God for myself and not what the culture, subculture of countercultures says, but as a prophet, I know God, and what is weak in me is made strong in Him.

Remember that prophets will defy the norms of their subculture. The very subculture that they grew up in. We must deal with right and wrong as we walk in and by faith. That's what coexisting is all about. Now we have become relevant. Relevant is a popular subculture term; it speaks of the ability to deal with the issues and times of the day but still use God as the barometer.

It is relevant because we were taught not to fear the hard questions and uncomfortable issues. It is relevant because being different and still being a normal person whose relationship with God is an uncompromising dedication to truth. It is relevant because we are unafraid of befriending sinners and sharing the gospel with them.

In 1 Corinthians 9:18, the great Apostle Paul wrote, "That he had become all things to everyone for the gospel." Paul showed us how he adapted his ministry to the situations of particular cultures, the Jews, the Gentiles, the weak, etc.

A variety of cultures, all existing simultaneously, to which Paul had to adapt at different times. This was the essence of the whole point of Paul's becoming all things to all men for the sake of the gospel.

We, to a man, knew his culture as it had changed to Christ, and he was adaptable to God's people.

Today in the Body of Christ, we have a big outer circle called "Kingdom Culture." This culture is formed by Christian people's theology, doctrine, and behavior. Paul calls it "the household of God" (Ephesians 2:19). Christians are chosen people (1 Peter 2:9) that have a specific calling in life. This is the most significant aspect of culture and forms the governing principles based on theology, doctrine, and behavior.

Then there is a smaller circle within the big one. It is the "Local, Contemporary Culture." This is the culture of your particular place of ministry. This is where we may find ourselves as prophets or other 5-fold ministry gifts. Our interaction with others will vary. This is where we are identified and start to function.

Finally, there is the smaller circle, the "Internal Subculture," of a particular group of believers. This circle includes the smallest number of people and has to do with a specific set of cultures, customs, expectations, etc., within a larger local contemporary culture.

The prophet again is the prime example as we are now within our specialized development ranks. The cultural behavior of the subculture may vary slightly from the broader culture, but they live within it.

Because of the differences in cultures, there tends to be some disagreement among Christians as to how (or how much) they should take on the lifestyle of their surrounding culture. That's understandable, and it is an accepted fact that we live with every day. Let's look at a few points to consider regarding contextualization.

Do not judge others who live in a different internal subculture. It's easy to cast aspersions on those who live or minister within a subculture typically viewed with suspicion, which is what many do to the prophetic ministry and within the Body of Christ. God has not called every prophet to cross-culture ministry.

A traditional church or a traditional ministry will be different from an inner-city church or ministry, just as we see in the gifting and the diversification of gifts. Paul wasn't trying to be a hip. Paul was making personal changes, even uncomfortable ones, "that by all means, I might save some" (1 Corinthians 9:22). Paul was, first of all "a servant to all, that I might win more" (1 Corinthians 9:19).

Like Paul, prophetic leaders must reach different prophetic subcultures, just as he reached different cultures. The subculture teachings minimize the potential danger that a half-crazed or misguided prophet could wrack upon a community.

May I say again that you need to be trained in your culture before you go into a cross-culture situation? Prophet, it is time out for you to claim that you are ready for cross cultural ministry on your way to the nations and you don't have a clue about your own personal culture.

I so wish Moses was here to instruct on this point. He would tell you it is critical. I want us to explore this and more, so you will understand that when I talk about my or anyone's culture, we can see how it affects some and does not affect others. I would also like to look within the Body of Christ. Do we realize that there are things that affect us that are birthed in the Body of Christ?

Let me be clear that yes, the Body of Christ affects our culture. Let's look at three different types of deception within the Body of Christ's culture and then reflect this to your particular culture. Prophet, let's get real. We do have some issues.

Let me introduce you to traditional deception. This is deception based on thinking that has been handed down from previous generations and accepted without question. May I say again, without question? Many well-meaning teachers, as well as parents, are responsible for this deception.

An example is that religion has associated poverty with godliness. To think you cannot prosper because a parent or loved one told you that no one in your family tree has ever prospered is a deadly deception. We now have a classic example of a concept that has been taught and handed down, just like cultural bias and, yes, even racism, all in the Body of Christ. This is the year 2022 and to say it is not alive and well in the Body of Christ is an insult to the intelligence of those who testify to this fact.

Doctrinal Deception is extremely powerful, especially when we talk about it from a cultural and Body of Christ standpoint. Let's keep talking about poverty. How many of us have been taught poverty that is supported because it is misrepresented in scripture and clearly taken out of context?

How many do you know who teach that "money is just plain evil." A reading of the Word will not say money is evil; it says the love of money is evil (I Timothy 6:10). Then there is the Jesus was poor teaching, so we are to be poor. Let's just ignore the fact that Jesus had a team of seventy. I'm sure they looked to him for pay because their families had to eat and live also.

Now let's pass this poor fact about Jesus upon our culture and claim it a doctrine. We can't find the fact He was totally poor. II Corinthians 8:9 says, *"That though he was rich, yet for our sakes, That Jesus became poor, is talking about Jesus on the cross, through His poverty you and I may become rich."* Question prophet? Has your culture taken this totally out of context and ran with it, or is the teaching of your culture or subculture or even counter-culture conflicting with what I just shared?

Cultures are different, and the deception that is produced by the experiences of life is different. This is called experiential deception. Surely prophets, you remember when you went to the circus, and the elephants were small. The trainers could and would chain them will steel leg irons to keep them confined to a certain area.

We see as time goes on, the elephant grows. The leg irons should have been replaced with ropes and wooden stakes. Sometimes there were, and many times they were not. The large elephant could very easily break chains or ropes. This does not happen because the elephant is convinced that escaping is impossible. This is the mentality in the Body of Christ over issues such as money, customs, and traditions.

The same thing is true with our humanity based on our culture. Our experiences of life have confined all of us. My question is, do we ignore all of our experiences, especially the ones that have confined us, and do we accept the experiences of another culture sight unseen? Well, let's see, Moses did not and he is a great example to follow.

We must learn as prophets how to develop reaping strategies (Amos 9:13). The problem is when Prophets fail to communicate, when people, in general, fail to communicate, there is an issue. The issue of cultural differences and because of those differences, we cancel each other's effectiveness.

God wants you and I to prosper. In Deuteronomy 8:18, God gives us all the ability to be a success to accomplish His plan for each of our lives; Joshua 1:8 says, *"This Book of God's Law shall not depart from you."* Joshua says we are to meditate in it night and day. This is how we will be able to observe to do God's work as it is written. This is the key to being prosperous and having great success.

As a prophet, Joshua learned that success occurred as a result of his behaving wisely and acting prudently. For a prophet, success occurs when we study to develop skills and understanding of the assignment that God has given us.

The more we learn how to steward our gifts, the more God can use us. I feel it is ludicrous to go to a country, state, or region as a prophet sent to the nations and not even know or be aware of my own culture, much less someone else's culture. Prophets, we steward by using God's plan of giving and managing, which will shift us into an anointing transference.

For a prophet, this means recognizing God and His laws, and blessing Him with your substance, worship, and response to authority. I know you know; we all know prophets who have been blessed by God outwardly in the presence of their enemies. Prophets, God has a plan! Now is the time! The culture in many churches today softly conveys the idea that it is more spiritual to be poor than to be rich.

Leaders, especially prophets, cannot speak passionately about Kingdom issues and then slip into an apologetic, Dr. Jekyll type tone as the unpleasant topic off money is to be discussed." We are the bridges of cultures; we must become all things to all people. Let's start the process by understanding what affects one person may or may not affect another person. We must be sensitive to this.

CHAPTER 2

"MY CULTURE AND HOW IT AFFECTS ME AND NOT YOU"

Marketers look at the culture of a particular race of people. They develop commercials about the lifestyle. You are a prophet, and you are sent to a specific people; they may look like you or not. Moses is sent to His people, and he is a stranger among and to his people.

The standard that marketers use is made up of assumptions of the creators who make money, if they are correct. This is why kids will line up for hours for that particular item that has been targeted at them. This is what makes a "cool factor" as people spend money.

The point here is to understand what makes one react to their culture's norms a certain way. Some of you may not respond to the following examples of cultural behavior. Does that make you wrong? Does that make you insensitive?

The key is to understand that culture behaves based on events that have happened and are happening. Culture is influenced by behavior. This behavior is based on laws and attitudes within a society's belief system.

Prophets now take the following culture tests and see if they relate to or apply to you in any way. Apostle Paul says in 1st Corinthians 9 that I have become all things to all men, that they are saved.

Prophets, there is the challenge to follow the example of Paul. This is the foundation of understanding really how tough our job is, and our dependence upon God is vital.

I now will list some situations that people of different cultures may or may not face. There are many factors that people of certain cultures respond to. Prophet, rest assured that you will face or be exposed to some of these situations in your ministry.

We all should know these can vary by things like race, education, laws, and, yes again, the belief system of such people. As you look at these tests, be open and honest with yourself and see if they apply to you or if you can relate to them.

Let's consider Paul, the outsider who had to become all things to all me. This means he had to know how to relate and communicate. The ability of Paul to do these things was God-given, and I can't help but wonder if we are all at certain levels in our ability to relate and communicate.

My point here is that we talk about how we should be. We reflect on what the Ekklesia should look like and how it should be. As a prophet who has traveled and been in various cultures, let me present this test to you. Prophet, let us see if you can relate to any of these. Have fun, but please understand how serious this is. Here we go:

1. Something has happened that you know and react to as being unfair. Action to correct the situation is little to none. You are angry and need to show that you can remain calm because you're aware of how you are being labeled.

This is how you feel. The very sign of your raising your voice in a given situation gets you culturally labeled, even if you are right. The question prophet, is can you understand how this person may feel, and can you relate to it?

2. You walk into a store and make a purchase. There are others in the store. You now make a purchase. You will not leave the store until you get a bag and receipt.

The size of your purchase does not matter; you must have a bag and a receipt. You know you may be stopped coming out of the store. The question prophet, is can you understand how this person may feel, and can you relate to it?

3. The area you live in is dominated by a different culture than you may be. You walk into the store, and you feel safe by going out of your way to make a point of approaching staff first as you walk into the store.

You ask a question in a friendly manner, even if you already know the answer. The sales staff now has a feel for who you are, and they feel safer around your presence. The question prophet, is can you understand how this person may feel, and can you relate to it?

4. Prophet, in this example, the person is traveling, and it's an area that the person may not be from.

The reality is that it may be a sundown town, in which everything closes at sundown.

You are in a country-type atmosphere, and you are super reluctant to stop because you are different, and you feel super uncomfortable because you are low on gas. Your perception is this, night has settled in, and you do not want to stop at a local country store where everyone knows everyone; it is not an appealing option.

You pray that you can make it to a larger gas station in a more developed, more lighted area. The question, prophet, is, can you understand how this person may feel, and can you relate to it?

5. Imagine being pulled over by the police; you know it is wise to keep your insurance and registration current and easy to find. This will help you not make sudden moves or trigger unwarranted actions from the police. The question, prophet, is, can you understand how this person may feel, and can you relate to it?

6. A father has taught his sons how to drive after they have got their licenses; that same father now teaches them how to remain calm and display quality behavior in their dealings with the police if stopped.

The purpose of this behavior is not to have his sons deemed a threat and make it home alive. The father has given his sons quality training and yet he still worries. The question prophet, is can you understand how this person may feel, and can you relate to it?

7. A guy is meeting with executives or high-ranking officials where appropriate attire would be business casual for others; he wears full business attire. This guy has found that if he dresses formally, he gets more attention, eye contact, head-nodding, and enthusiasm during conversations.

This happens consistently to him. He notices that his words are not enough. His reputation and credentials are of the highest. He is the only person of his culture, and he finds that his attire overrides their initial perception of who he is or how they think he should be. He finds it tiring to have to go above and beyond constantly just to be taken seriously. The question prophet, is can you understand how this person may feel, and can you relate to it?

Some of you may realize it, and some of you may not, but until you can put yourself in that situation, you will never really understand what being all things to all people is about. I have just listed seven situations by a culture of people that feel they have to make certain adjustments even now in 2022 as I write this.

We all know there are cultures that do not have these issues. I see this as a prophet clearly, and there is the reality we seem, more often than not, to prefer to ignore. How we do this varies, and we all have a way that we have devised, even if it means looking and saying absolutely nothing. Prophet, this is the mentality we have.

How would you think Apostle Paul would relate to or even feel toward these situations? Let us now open ourselves up to cross cultures and put ourselves in the places of these people. We are being sent to places that these people oftentimes live in. This is the real reality of being prepared and respecting a culture whether or not you agree with it or not.

The reality of dealing with impossibilities is commonplace within the depths of working in cross-culture ministry. Impossibilities to us are commonplace to God. We must understand that they exist and will not go anywhere because this is the world that God created for us.

Today sit back and think when was the last time you were in a meeting of leaders, and the call for unity was echoed within the meeting. We all reflected on how awesome God was and what needed to happen through God. We all made decrees and talked about how we would do it and what it was really going to take.

Once this was done, a common theme of cultural differences showed up yet again. Some of us could very well be a part of the cultural issues described in this chapter. The reality is that some of you, as you read this, struggle to imagine being a part of that culture where the status quo shows up again.

You are supposed to be working with others to bring change, and you find out that the meeting was a well-meaning remnant representation of what we could have, but we fail to achieve. Prophet, you must bring the needed anointing for change, which will be your greatest challenge.

Let's take a personal count of how many of us can relate to this. The issue of us as prophets seems to be how we may be looked at differently because we are of a different culture. This chapter was not for the reader to point fingers at one group of people and ignore them. This chapter is for you, the prophet, to get a feeling of how different cultures of people are affected in the same environment, but by different ways.

Prophet, God has not called you to ignore the difficult situations and shy away from them with generic generalizations. Prophet, this is real life, in the real world we live in, and this is a real challenge put before us all. Prophet, do we really want to be God's tools of unity, or do we want to turn our heads?

DO WE REALLY WANT UNITY IN THE BODY OF CHRIST?

Let's look at the Body of Christ. Do we really want unity? What type of examples are each of us as prophets projecting? We talk well, but we do not act well. In 2022, some will still ask if Cross-cultural and multicultural ministry and worship are necessary.

They belittle the prophet and tell us to stay in our own cultural circles. They speak loudly with their actions, so why not stay in our cultural circles? Let's identify who "they" are.

The ones who constantly throw stones at us and yet specialize in cover-up art. They speak life to our faces and become our biggest and most dangerous enemy within the Body of Christ.

They are the ones who bond with you at the meeting, if only to find out what you have, judge your spiritual level, and evaluate whether you are called or not, according to their standards. Please meet your "they"; we all have them, and it's how we handle them which is the key.

Let me continue as they say we have different national and cultural backgrounds, we already know that, and they suggest that maybe we should stay where we feel comfortable and respected. This is not always spoken but implied. We see it at selected meetings when it's time to eat, break, and even fellowship. We all seem to stay or migrate to where we are comfortable.

This is a social interaction that we already practice. Welcome to the Body of Christ today. This is not to say that we do not extend our hand in fellowship or show ourselves friendly. We all have been involved in these situations, and it does not take much to visualize this.

My question is to those who seek the same unity I do; how do we do it? Prophets, we have to be able to envision a day where we will have one faith, believing in one Bible. We are talking to you, prophet, about cross-cultural ministry, and the reality is it is a monumental task for 2022 and beyond. The issue of cross-cultural ministry among the remnants is debatable and varies.

The reality of ethnic boundaries is real and can't be ignored, especially by members of that particular culture. We are all human and subject to be rational social actors of our culture and others. The reality is that a slight bit of modification will take work. Let me welcome you to the Body of Christ yet again and the issues of cultures.

Within the Body of Christ, we have seemingly failed to understand that our intentions and actions will be consistent with the cultural climate. How many of us can envision a day when God will send your best friend ever, and they will be from another culture, and if not for them, you would be lost? Does this happen today? Sure it does, but how many of us does it happen to and for? Let's be honest here. The number is low.

So many of you, as prophets, read this and may think about how you have tried to bond with those from another culture. Was there a personal cultural pullback towards you, or were you doing the pullback?

The reality of you doing it for the sake of doing it did not figure in your actions, especially if you never understood the importance of the moment.

Here is my thought. Prophet, have you noticed that our world is transforming into a multicultural society due to technology, health, theology, and visionaries from various walks of life, including ministry? The prophet is tasked today to be among those whom God has called to unite multicultural groups.

Prophets, the Lord's Supper has always presented a picture of how a relationship with God can lead to unity among His people. The Bible is an excellent example of bringing people together of different cultures. Do you struggle, prophet, to deal with your brothers and sisters of different cultures regularly?

I am presenting an example here, but when was the last time we saw a man or woman of God, knew who they were, and went to eat with them despite being of a different culture? Did we move past the awkwardness of maybe not having little to no relationship with them to start the process of building one?

Most of us will find some self-acceptable answer; others will struggle. The fact that I need to raise the question reflects a much bigger issue.

Prophet, what I am speaking of is not easy for congregations, groups, ministries, or individuals. Language differences, concerns, and cultural norms must be overcome. As we have been assigned, this is not easy for the prophets, yet we still struggle to understand the basic tenants of personal cross-cultural ministry.

Let us, as prophets, understand that the beauty of the anointing will unite ethnic backgrounds in unity, but the work must be put in. Within the Body of Christ, and I will discuss this later, if you disrespect or make one feel uneasy or do not understand how to acknowledge a leader, it will easily lead to a total downfall, especially when different cultures are involved.

The prophet's ability to go to the nations is critical to the work of the Prophet, still today. Let's consider some important facts. Many ministries you may go to are greatly influenced by location and culture. This includes overseas also. We must consider a strong sense of pride for any given ethnicity or culture. In other words, have some respect.

Within that ethnicity, there are subcultures and countercultures. So understand that God is now deploying you to work in a cross-cultural environment. Prophet, if God has sent you, the expectation is real despite what you see or are a witness to.

Experience is always good to deploy with your knowledge of other denominational cultures in any given area. Understand that there may be an implicit fear of various cultures even in the theatre of your cross-cultural assignment.

I am simply saying you need to learn something about the area you are going to. Favor can be your friend because you took the time to learn about your assignment. Yes, this is work, and for the now generation prophet, are you willing to do it?

What does it take to motivate the prophet today to push yourself into understanding and pursuing diversity? There is a reality here, and you will need to realize it. You will never win people into unified multicultural worship unless you respect them.

I have learned that you can respect someone and disagree with them all at the same time. I may worship differently, but I respect their cultural diversity as it still reflects that we are all Christians. We are the now generation seers, brothers, and sisters in Christ, failing to realize that.

Multicultural worship does not happen automatically; this type of work, I submit, is done by respecting who God has in positions of authority and learning how to work with them to accomplish a goal. Prophet, we all need to realize that is part of our personal development. How many of us have failed or are failing?

Prophets, there is a way to handle yourself respectfully when you are presented with traditions that are not yours. When God sends you, this is a factor you will need to take into account sufficiently.

In 1 Corinthians 9:22, Apostle Paul speaks about becoming all things to all everyone. Prophet, we must see his motivation to accept the assignment God had given him and his will to be submissive to another culture and still be who he was to God.

Here is where many prophets or aspire to be prophets will brag about their credentials with a specific culture to spread the message of their special cultural gift. We spend more time trying to impress people and our peers rather than understanding how serious the privilege and opportunity of cross-cultural ministry really is. This is a small wonder. We have so many problems trying to come together.

Galatians 2:20 show us that Paul had completely abandoned his old self for Christ, and thus he was effective in working in cross cultures. Let me be clear; Paul by no means didn't try to compromise to fit in. I often wonder do prophets feel that way. We could also ask that question to the Body of Christ. Prophet, are you willing to forgo traditions and familiar comforts in order to reach any audience, Jewish or non-Jewish, black, green, or white?

Prophet, you need to remember that the next time God sends you to a specific audience, what and how will you find common ground with them? Paul knew how to behave in a Hebrew or Jewish household. He could become my brother for the sake of the gospel.

Many times as prophets sent to cross cultures, our ability is tested, especially in the art of needing to break the mold of our very own cultural traditional thinking.

The very act of worship helps form the faith of the people to whom God has sent you. A prophet to the nation sent to a cross-cultural will have to learn quickly that various faith backgrounds and religious traditions are precious experiences to those to who you are sent.

Prophet, you are the example. You must display your relationship with God to show that God has sent you to show them another way of success. Let me say that your attitude toward everything you see differently is essential. You're the one who is sent to connect and establish God in the manner He desires.

Today prophets, you will deal with multiple standards of theology. The non-denomination, or denomination, and of course, the traditions of the church, group, or ministry. Today, we see that many pastors have visions for multicultural churches and adhere to the worship customs of the core group of that church.

When I say core group, you can imagine I'm talking about dominant families, influential families, financially strong families, and members, just to name a few. Many times there are essential members in a multicultural church especially.

The point here is that you must understand that going to do cross-cultural ministry will vary as the multicultural church ministry will. Every church or group clearly has its own identity. Prophet, you must understand that God has sent you with your own special identity also.

Prophet, your ability to handle yourself is a critical point I must stress. A handshake or a light hug will demonstrate God's acceptance and a spirit of unity. The eyes are on you, and you must know how to handle and protect yourself at the same time.

Let's face it, within the prophetic community, there is division because we are groups of counter cultures within the prophetic culture. Our exposure to the fact should help us strive to be aware of a need to close the gaps between cultures. Our experience should teach us and not separate us. When we do not grow, we help foster cultural issues like racism and sexism. These are issues we must deal with.

CHAPTER 4

RACISM AND SEXISM IN THE PROPHETIC MINISTRY

Prophet, while this is a touchy topic, let's discuss it anyway. When we think about racism, there is no state, no geographical region of this country or world that is immune to racism, which means there is no ministry immune to racism. The very culture of racism is totally out of control today.

Racism is a culture of social domination. This culture thrives in alliance with other forms of unjust domination such as sexism, class, and political domination. Racism is fiercely resistant to change.

The culture believes it is right and has reason to feel that way. Societies seek self-preservation and willingly embrace racism rather than lose their 'power.' We are born into this at all levels of society. Why would it be in the prophet? As long there is a culture of different perspectives, we can account for racism.

Racism hurts and humiliates its victims. Racism creates in oppressors a false sense of superiority; and is profoundly painful for those it demeans. The problem is we have this in the Body of Christ, and we struggle to deal with it effectively.

The prophetic is a part of the Body of Christ, and there is an unspoken reality that in some places under the banner of Christ, we won't be accepted because we are of an outside culture. While that is a shame, it is a reality.

As prophets, we seem to have ignored our cultural decline. Today we see prophets looking for someone to hate, blame and tear down; we see prophets not growing. This is a sure sign of our unfaithful behavior and cultural decay.

We see divisions within our ranks, where things like skin color and nationality derail opportunities for some prophets, and ones hide behind the banner "in the name of Jesus." The issue is real, yet the problem is not relevant in some remnants churches and ministries where there has been work done to understand the importance of cross relationships. The point here is that one place is one too many.

We also see the respect of person, in who can and who will minister to certain individuals. That heart of deceit with prophets is alive and well among our prophetic ranks, and we ignore it within ourselves because we want to be in the crowd of our gifting.

How many prophets who practice this refuse to repent because they feel a God-given right to tear their brother or sister prophet down to make a name for themselves? 1 Corinthians 14:31 says that prophets' spirits are obedient to prophets meaning the authorized use of God's Word.

Today we as a Body of Christ rather look at the color of their skin first, but the Word was and still is the most important thing. We who call ourselves prophets in this New Testament generation can't ignore this and must adhere to it no matter the color of a prophet's skin. It's a shame to judge someone sent of God by the skin color and allow that to determine if that person or prophet is of God.

We, the now generation prophets fall into the trap of easy to condemn; it's difficult to absorb, much less confront, such blatant racism. Why is there so much blatant racism among the prophets who profess a calling for God? What has the prophetic community taught, and what has been imparted to us? All of us are products of someone, somewhere.

But as we look at the prophetic ministry, what about the subtler forms of racism we encounter? Do we hold ourselves accountable, prophets? As a prophet, your faith should not allow you to assume immunity to sin.

Apostle Paul wrote Romans 3:23, which says, *"All have sinned and fall short of the glory of God."* In Isaiah 46:6, the prophet gives, *"All our righteous deeds are like a filthy garment."*

"There is no special line separating good from evil. The reality is there is no class either; it is what is in the heart of each one of us. Searching for the best of our hearts, there remains an un-uprooted small corner of evil. This is true for us as prophets." We have all sinned.

The enemy wants to lock us in sin, and our only out is through and by Jesus. Compared to God's law, our standards are far more inconsistent and skewed to favor prophets or people you felt you could relate to based on their skin color or personal personality acceptance.

Let's consider that most of us as prophets have been practicing such consistent moral failing in our daily lives for years, becoming mundane and routine. We talk about being called to the nations and fail to realize the different cultures will present this same challenge that we need to know how to overcome within ourselves first.

We, as the prophets of this generation, have become immune to race-based discrimination and sexism because we don't think it's in the prophetic ministry.

For most of us, this season has illuminated a need to understand and repent for racism and systemic injustice and listen to others' experiences and perspectives. This is not just for African Americans and Native Americans but for all races and creeds.

We must realize God is sending us to nations that are operating deeply ingrained in prejudice and racism. God is sending His prophets to people with hearts that need to change; that's why your prophetic message is critical.

God is using you, male or female, sending you to a place where you may be the only person that looks like you. You will be noticed, and people will question why are you here.

Among leaders, our snap judgments reveal a layer of our prejudices as prophets that have us relying on associated norms from fictional television shows to news reports and not God. These prophetic stereotypes, accurate and inaccurate, attract us to repulsive qualities and images seemly before we confer with God.

For some people, your prophetic birthing will be in their season of divine connection, and you're the connection to a deeper meaning and understanding with God. So you must be led by God and not a perception or the color of someone's skin.

Prophets, if those in your circle of relationships mostly look like you, and have no divine authority to spur your empowerment, then who will speak in your life and challenge you to be accountable that they sensed some racism in a remark, assumption, or interaction?

These prophets like you probably share the same blind spots and, therefore, probably would not pick up on implicit racism. That's what we have going on today in the prophetic realm.

As a prophet, understanding and respecting diversity in your gift and who has it or does not have it could help you receive and process a suggestion of racism without attacking or dismissing the other prophetic voices.

Regardless of who provides it, this is the foundation essence of prophetic empowerment. This is the authentic prophetic culture.

To take this to another level, we also clearly see sexism, especially in the prophetic ministry there is an effort to preserve the subordination of female prophets and prevent what they call the feminization of Prophetic and Apostolic ministry.

Traditional Denominational doctrine has produced Christian spokespeople who make much of the fact that Jesus was incarnated as a man and not a woman. They say his sexual identity confirms the "natural" order of male dominance. While it does sound somewhat silly, it is taken as fact.

Thank God we see the focus of the ministry of the female prophets leaning more towards the solidification of gender equality and the elimination of sexism. Be advised there is still significant undercover sexism not just in mainline denominations but in the Body of Christ as a whole, especially for female prophets.

We see several factors to support this, such as

(1) Over the past twenty years, for example, female prophets have increased but not without men's and women's opposition to female leadership in the Body of Christ. Especially those who God calls to be Apostles.

(2) The struggle of female prophets to be ordained or, in some cases, denied as prophets is not only seemly a political process, but the struggle involves socio-political-theological issues of sexism, such as whether or not women are capable of fulfilling the roles men have dominated.

(3) Some see and prescribe to the perception of inferiority, as they can't lead groups of prophets, much less God's people.

We live in a season of destructive unbalance in families, as some teach and establish a dominance that disrespects women. There is no relevant cause to hide the fact that this is alive and well; it thrives in more prophetic circles than it should.

We see female prophets who speak the Word of God, and it's suddenly and blatantly disrespected. We see the same Word spoken by a male, and it's accepted. Many times Prophetess Cox and I have seen this.

There are the men who do not want a woman to pray for them, much less speak into their life. This behavior did not just manifest one day; it goes back to their background. The blame has to be equally shared.

Men have not taught their sons to respect women, and the same women who, at great cost to themselves to nurture their children, some for various reasons and circumstances, have allowed their sons to be conditioned to violence and disrespect.

Sons who became men have been allowed to be taught to become the kind of men in whom compassion and concern have been diminished to the point of disrespect simply because the prophet may be a woman.

This is a culture and a dangerous one. They also silently demonstrate to their daughters to be de-feminized, incomplete human beings that does not represent the true nature of the order of God's people.

Today we see many prophetic women in the Body of Christ. Some are married. Some are not. We, as prophets, can no longer allow religion and tradition to keep women shut down and repressed. Your sex does not matter; do you have the assignment from God to accomplish it?

Prophetess Deborah in Judges 4 was sought after when Barak was afraid to go on the assignment God gave him. In Judges 4:21, remember a lady named Jael, who, with a tent peg and a hammer in her hand, killed the king that Barak was supposed to kill.

Numbers 27:1–7 teaches us that Apostolic fathers need to release the daughters to prophesy, bless them and give them confidence, especially in this day a time. Scripture says then came near the daughters of Zelophehad, stood before Moses, who was seated the high priest and other leaders of the assembly by the door of the tent of meeting.

They said their dad was dead, but they were to get possession of his property. Their dad had no sons. They were clear as they spoke to Moses and other leaders and said give us our fathers possessions.

Moses brought their case before the Lord. God spoke to Moses and told him that the daughters of Zelophehad told the truth and to give them what was theirs. We see now that there should not be any prophetess who feels defeated because she is a prophet. God has no respective person because He is a just God!

As prophets, we collectively mourn wicked assault after wicked assault because of racism and sexism. As prophets, we can't deny this sin. We continue to hurt our brother and sister prophets and grieve the Holy Spirit, and we miss knowing God in critical ways as He continues to reveal in those who value humanity, many of whom we disrespect because they are different.

Those who deny others because they are of different skin color, heritage, or different sex will never know God in totality to accomplish the assignment on their life. They refuse to change. The reality, prophets, is that we will not see real change until we take responsibility for our own personal racism and sexism. Then we can help others. Scripture clearly does not give us room to proclaim innocence.

Too many of us as prophets have self-fulfilling prophecies that are hollow and limited by our limited intellect and not God. The same concept can describe how a statement may alter actions and become true. In situations of today's prophetic, we have many individuals act based on our self-fulling views.

Many of today's prophets participate in self-fulfilling prophecies where prophets justify their prejudices toward members of other cultures and ethnic groups. Have you ever heard statements like, "I don't want those people here because they only stick to themselves?" This sounds chauvinistic, and there is a reason why on both sides of the issue.

The self-fulfilling prophecy is an attitude-adjusted prophecy birthed in a culture of small-mindedness and hate. You're a prophet, and your mindset may be an example to influence other people to perceive you positively.

Prophets who tend to be caught in negative self-fulfilling prophecies often suffer from low self-esteem where they act overly critical and tend to make snap judgments on others, especially their peers.

This prophet's pessimistic view of the world leads to a vicious cycle, where their negative mindset strengthens their self-fulfilling prophecies. This strongly holds a culture of racism and sexism in the prophetic. This is a dangerous culture in the prophetic, and many refuse to believe they are part of it. We all have prejudices that hold us in this realm.

Prejudice in any form, racial or social, is destructive and costly to society and the Body of Christ. Today, as prophets, we see social prejudice is accepted by society, and few realize its destructive force. It kills motivation and forces prophets to give up and accept failure. Joseph was one such prophet.

He could have accepted failure. His family's culture affects him and shows why our relationship with God is priceless. Again to understand Cross-culture, we need to understand our family culture. Keep reading and imagine if you walked into this type of drama.

CHAPTER 5

THE EFFECTS OF CULTURE, THE PROPHET AND HIS FATHER

Every prophet is affected by the culture of their background. Being a prophet in this world is a challenge. Can you imagine being the father of a prophet? The reality of fatherhood may be devalued in our society today as we see many single-parent homes. Let us make no small issue of the importance of fatherhood; it is critical and often reflected later in life if it was available or not.

The blessing of a father can mean the world to a child. The biblical days offer us an example to appreciate. Here is the culture of a family with one of God's greatest prophets. Take time to follow the life of Joseph. He is a seer, a prophet, and a leader, and he becomes the greatest Prophetic Steward the world has ever known. His father, Jacob, loved him greatly.,

We look at the culture of a family as we look at Jacob, and his life will show you a man who is dealing with multiple issues. Jacob represents a lot of fathers today. Some things have happened because of decisions through the generations, and your family is known to be a certain way. This is what we refer to as your family culture.

Maybe, to the prophetic fathers, things have happened in your family, and you are broken, angry, and mad, and as the leader, all the heat of what's wrong in your family is upon you. You're a father, and to accept the good, you must be willing to accept the not-so-good also. Welcome to the burden of leadership; you have earned it with fatherhood.

Jacob is the father and, like fathers of today, whose example of a father is the key to his blessings on your life. In the day of Jacob, a father's blessings meant the world. Genesis 49 reveals the mindset and mentality of Jacob. He is a patriarch, and his final blessing was important as a practical matter of inheritance rights. We see Jacob, the father of Joseph, here giving his final blessings, and here we start to understand the complex nature of a prophet's Father and how it affects that prophet.

Again lets us go to Genesis 49 as we witness a father who knows he is dying, and this father, Jacob, wants his sons to gather for his Patriarchal Blessing upon their lives. The culture of this family is revealed as Jacob speaks. The sons gather, and we see the father's influence played out in detail as Jacob rebukes Reuben for sleeping with one of his concubines in verse 3. In verse 6, we see another angry rebuke from Jacob against Simeon and Levi.

Jacob speaks to them with great anger. He expresses that they are violent and wants himself and the family to be separate from them! He is a man dying, and he is angry. This is a strange concept to us in this generation, or is it?

The brothers gather, and we see Jacob speaking his final words to them. He is angry, hurt, and disgusted with what they did to the men of Shechem and how they treated his favorite son Joseph. The drama and beliefs are now on display for this family. The background here is that Jacob had lived many years of his life and thought Joseph was dead. As a father, and a parent, he mourns in the process of learning of his son's death; he blames Levi and Simeon primarily as the lead conspirators against Joseph. Can you imagine the thoughts in the mind of Joseph?

This is a family issue and what you see is the pain and disappointment from the father being played out on his death bed. He refuses to bless Joseph's brothers as he has lived a miserable life watching them in their inherited values. Values that Jacob does not seem to understand.

Jacob had a wife named Leatha, with whom he had a daughter named Dinah, who was raped. Jacob is upset by how the men of Shechem were treated, as they were deceived and killed as a nation by his sons Levi and Simeon. The brothers are now embarrassed and imagine the uneasy feeling as the patriarch of the family is dying, and he is disgusted in his final moments. This is a big deal with the culture's customs as Jacob fought for his dad's blessings; we don't see much of that today.

We have devalued the fathers in ways only society can and continues to identify for us. Sometimes we are referred to as sperm donors and other names because of the family status and situations. Little do we realize that the culture of our families is dictating something that we need to break off our lives. Keep reading and look to see if your family's culture is reflected. Have you realized how much Joseph lost much of his life experience with his dad? What sustained Joseph was his relationship with God.

This has been a lifetime, and even now, as he has reconciled, there are still issues with his brothers, and the cost of what their drama cost him is still evident. So many of us today never realize that we are going into cultures with our family's issues. While we don't think we may need a father's blessing in our culture today because we feel we know things that we do not. We must face that elements of our now day generation have taken us away from the fact that God is still in charge and honor that father and thy mother commandment still mean just what it says despite your situation.

Can you imagine speaking to your dad on his deathbed, and he is upset with you because of what you did to your brother, who was gifted differently than you? Your dad is dying, and you can't fix the issue as time is running out. You lied and deceived your dad; can you relate to that?

Prophet, the lesson here is to get it right; whatever the case may be with your dad, do your part and get it right. The reality of life is, would you rather live with guilt or grief? Prophet, also be aware that you can have guilt and grief because you did not make things right. I am sharing this with you; like many who will read this, you have far-reaching issues in your family that will affect you. Joseph as a seer, conducts himself in an honorable way.

Picture this situation as the sons of Jacob are around his bed, and they are dealing with decisions and consequences of those decisions. There are some hard-established cultural facts to consider. Jacob, as their father, was not a loving father. He openly communicated his great love for his son Joseph above and beyond what he expressed for his other sons. They knew Joseph was his favorite of Jacob, and yes, they were jealous of the fact.

As a father, Jacob did nothing to make this situation right. Jacob loved Joseph so much because Racheal was his mom, and she was the love of Jacob's life. Remember Jacob worked 14 years to be able to marry Racheal and Joseph, the seer, the prophet was the love child he had with Racheal.

This is why the jealousy and evil they did toward Joseph were so unforgivable for Jacob, and this ruined his family relationships until his death. Looking at this, Jacob felt deceived and disrespected as a father because of the lies his sons told him about Jacob. The other side of this is that his handling of Joseph in a deliberate show of favoritism was what caused his sons to act the way they did.

Welcome to the prophetic years of not being able to fit in and not understanding why some hate you so bad or resent you. Yes, you are affected by it, and why you go on your cross-culture assignment, many of you will have a deposited experience like Joseph did.

This situation lingered for years. This is a family matter that has consequences that affect the entire family. Jacob's decisions to do what he has done have followed him. The manifestations of his decisions are shown now on his death bed in anger, bitterness, disappointment, and scorn for the sons he should have blessed.

Fathers, and prophets, who are fathers, look at Jacob; he has to have guilt in his life. He has driven his sons with selfishness to commit a travesty against his family. You'll be hard-pressed to tell me that is not on his mind either. Jacob has pushed his family to take advantage of a weakness in two different situations.

There is the rape of Dinah, the deception of men of Shechem, and the killing of them by the deception of Levi and Simeon, and Jacob knew this and set silence. He knew it was wrong and said nothing. The second thing to consider is that the behavior of these identical two sons was the push to kill Joseph, and they would have if it had not been for Reuben, their older brother. Let's look at the fact that, like many fathers, they transfer their guilt to other family members. We see this in the life of Jacob. Let's shout out to families and prophetic dads who may be a father. Have you transferred your guilt or hate to someone, and you are blaming them for what you may have refused to take responsibility for?

Prophets, there is another issue to look at: if you Jacob knew your son was dead, or thought your son was dead was nobody, what was the reason you did not search for him with your sons who convinced you he was dead? A loving father would have been grieved, but he wanted to get his son and give him a proper burial. Jacob, how do you as a father not follow up on this? This was your son, and you refuse to follow up on his death; prophets, what's wrong with the family then and today?

Returning to Jacob, look at the family damage done through the generations. His mother, Rebecca, is a trickster, and Jacob has set a standard for his sons; in the reality that he robbed Esau out of his birthright with Isaac, deception and trickery were inherited by his sons, and now he lays on his deathbed cursing them. Sometimes you need to look at yourself before you curse and criticize others. Jacob was the father of one of God's most gifted prophets, yet he still puts his family in danger because he does not realize his accountability to God, his family, or himself.

Finally, there is a culture in your life that has to be broken; just like there is a culture in Jacobs's life, there is one in yours, and even if you are not a prophet but you are a dad, realize that when a culture destroys your life and in turn it destroys the life others, then there is a sign that the culture must be broken.

Simeon and Levi did not become like they were by themselves; they were a product of their culture. There are some things that, despite our situation, need to be broken from our lives. We are on our way to the nations and we must change our thought life. This book is designed to prepare you for the storm and falsehoods you will encounter in cross-cultural ministry. Prophets, you must understand your faith is a cult to unbelievers. So be willing to endure prophetic crushing along the way.

CHAPTER 6

PROPHETIC CRUSHING; THE DEATH OF A PROPHET'S WISDOM

My prophetic friend, there are a few things in life you can count on that affect every prophet. This does not matter if that prophet is male or female. This does not matter if that prophet is black, white, native American, or of any race. Let us realize that your assignment is cross-cultural, and we need the training.

Since race is not a factor, culture is, and see that it does not matter as every prophet everywhere has seasons in their life that they are overwhelmed, seasons that everything in their life goes wrong. Your call upon your life may be somewhat different but rest assured you will deal with this process, especially if you're on the way to the nations.

You have done what you have been asked, given of yourself and your resources and all that seems to happen in your life is constant issues that crush and devalue you on the most personal of levels. Did you ever consider that there may be a need to distance yourself from your environment?

You accepted the calling, and the result has been ridicule, abandonment, and constant critiques from friends, family, and those you felt you could have counted on to support your decision. Every prophet who God will use will be crushed to the point that your personal wisdom will die to the will of God. This process will happen quickly if you surrender. I spoke on this in my introduction.

Prophetic crushing is a process experienced by prophets that test your ability to endure the struggle you find that is active in your life. Prophetic crushing helps you understand the historical value of your life issues with the priorities and values it brings. Do you see how the study of culture is needed?

Prophetic crushing exposes you to a new awareness of the ambiguities of life. Prophetic crushing is another word for prophetic processing that opens the prophet up to understanding life's uncertainties. It's the struggles and the drama that makes you feel many times that God is not with you.

Prophetic crushing exposes you to cultures that learn differently than you do; it creates countercultures that reveal you to areas that are beyond your normal level of wisdom. Please notice that this is an ongoing process within your life.

Many prophets would not go through a season of crushing to acquire the mental elevation needed for effective prophetic operation. Prophet, when you are crushed, you must believe that God is taking you through it for his benefit, or you will become disillusioned and feel sorry for yourself.

The missing element that destroys prophets is not understanding God's timing in the process of his crushing of the prophet's life. I will share more on this on the principle of the wheat and tares in the next chapter.

We, as prophets, are the seeds of God's intentions. Amos 3:7 says surely He does nothing without telling His secrets to His servants, the prophets. The ability of the prophet to engage in a relationship with God is evident in the level of crushing and pain we suffer in our personal lives. Think about our disappointments and our personal failures that become a public shame to others, but the fact is that God has no shame. God is not concerned about how others see us when He is crushing and processing our lives.

In Hosea chapter 1, we see God has His prophet Hosea marry a woman who was a harlot, or today we would call her a prostitute. God was not concerned about how they talked about his prophet. God was concerned about developing His prophet as the earthly wisdom of Hosea died as he was crushed in the process of God allowing the reconciling Israel back to himself. Can you see what God had put in Hosea was necessary for His purposes with Israel? What God had in His prophet, Hosea, was more important than local idle gossip. What God has in you is more important than someone's self-righteous evaluation of you.

To understand this is to understand that when you feel you are off course in your life, you're really on course. This is trusting God and knowing that you are the exponent of His plan. Think about this, the only way up is to first be down and then ascend.

Prophet, we see Jesus say, "I have come that you would have life and have it more abundantly." The cost of that life was His death. Prophetic crushing takes us down a path of opposites. The wisdom we operate in is null and void; we accept the wisdom of

God. Prophetic crushing is personal; it births pain, and that pain often hurts. That pain puts us in situations that often seem unfair because God has exposed us to this experience for His purposes.

Prophet, have you ever had a private moment in a public place? Those of you who have, understand how God pushes you to front street and exposes your deposited experience. The point here is that to have a crop or harvest, you must disrupt the soil of development. Sometimes the weeds of life have to be pulled out of your life, and you must be retooled, repositioned, or even refocused to bring forth a harvest.

Prophetic crushing is the process that brings change to a prophet's life. This is a necessary prophetic function of private, sometimes secret pain that so many of us have become masters at hiding and dodging the process. As prophets, we often want to hide our fears; we want to project the image of a super prophet, and yet within the Word of God, there were no super prophets, only human beings who were gifted and still walked in an abundance of faults. This is a major reason we don't have the needed prophets who will listen and obey God today. Too many times, our prophetically gifted want to be entertainers instead of who God intends for us to be.

Prophetic crushing is often a slow, painful death to the prophet's ideas and cultural wisdom. Welcome to being prepped for the nations. Embrace the mentality. This is why the prophet takes time to develop because without knowing or realizing, we will fight the process of being prophetically crushed for servitude as a prophet. Prophetic crushing as God bruises us His prophets. This is throughout our life process on different levels.

Can you see God, prophet, as He puts us in places where we will deal with people who are different, difficult, and do not believe in you as a prophet, nor do they believe in God? Prophetic crushing makes you the prophet available and equipped to deal with them. We are God's prophets; we have survived the process of being prophetically crushed. As God's prophets, we should understand the cross-cultural ministry process, as we have been trained for it from day one of our lives.

Being prophetically crushed will allow you to be able to be used by God in a multitude of ways. The reason is that for a prophet, Prophetic Crushing will grow and push the glory of God out of you in any situation. Prophet, you must understand that if God never pushed you or allowed you to be tossed, you would never be the prophet you are now!

For many of us, becoming who God wants you to be will take more crushing within our lives. The more we become afflicted prophets, the more we will grow. I so wish Moses or Jeremiah were here right now. We must not let go of God, we must hold and become, and it is only through the suffering of being prophetically crushed. Yes, this will vary from prophet to prophet.

Some of you will experience being crushed by relationships, others will deal with sickness, some may have had to deal with being violated, and then some have been publicly humiliated for seemingly no reason.

Ephesians 3:20 says, *"Now unto him, now unto God who is able to do more than we may ask or think."* The reality prophet is we don't have a clue as to just how much God will do.

Prophet, understand that we are the seed of God's plan and His agenda, and we do not know the levels God will take us if we are prepared to go. We must trust God, as we are becoming the prophets God wants us to be. Again it is the timing of God that works; hand in hand with the crushing of God in a prophet's life.

Prophet, God will crush us as he closes doors before us, and He will crush us as He opens doors; this is why we don't have to question God. Look at where you came from and see that you have been crushed, yet there is still work to do. This is how to develop the mentality of a long-distance seer. Notice as you see God trusting you in the depth of His personal crushing of your life. The prophet Daniel was a great example of this. A prophet, seer, prophetess, watch-man, and apostle, must stand strong if you never back away, and you will eventually see yourself. This is the benefit of the wisdom that died in you.

There is a simple process we all have learned about, called the wheat and tares. We are crushed and yet it is with the issues of our life. The wheat and the tares grow together, and the difficult issues and people seem to stay in our lives and they have a great purpose. Chapter 7 will be a new challenge for some and a reflection for others. Yes, we are still dealing with culture.

You trusted God through the process and now be-cause you did not run, nor you did not hide. You saw it through, and now you see God doing things in your life that were impossible, and now you see the pos-sibilities as God trusts you because He has crushed you and your wisdom is dead, and you are fully sub-mitted to God. Let's now dig deeper with the wheat and tares.

CHAPTER 7

HOW WHEAT AND TARES DEVELOP PROPHETS FOR CROSS CULTURES

The culture of prophets is often debated and sometimes misunderstood. Jesus teaches the principle of the wheat and tares growing together. Prophets, our social groups, drive this process quicker and faster than God does.

This has been a staple lesson in all faiths that spreads the lesson that God will do the needed separating in due season. Let's now look at the prophet and see prophetic principles in understanding the wheat and tares.

Matthew 13:24-30 explains when the crop is planted, and there is a great satisfaction when no one looks, the enemy plants weeds or tares. The wheat grows and matures, and now we see also the tares as they have grown. The servants report to the master, and the master says to let them grow together until harvest time.

He wants them to wait until a specific time. The culture of prophetic development is based on the understanding that to get the best of what God has for you; it will take time. Prophet, we just discussed being crushed and yet the process of divine servitude of connecting cultures is serious business. Keep reading prophet. Time is an undisputed teacher that brings out the needed principles in one's life to allow them to be effective for God. Do you ever wonder why, in your environmental culture, you see prophets jump here and there?

Most prophets in various stages of development think that their dreams of prophetic visions will launch them to places of relevance that only God can take them. That is true, but the process of realizing the visions is a process that requires change, and that requires time. The prophetic culture is a culture that is based on specific times and principles executed in the life of every prophet.

Prophetically gifted people who fail to understand that time is your friend in the development process will do precisely and fail to develop. A prophet who wants to rush their development process will always fail.

What are examples, you ask? Let's look at the prophet who gets an assignment, walks away from the assignment, fails to accomplish it, then ignores the assignment. This is your recipe for failure.

Your assignment and zeal for a more significant, more high-profile task are competing just like the tares are now growing with the wheat. God is allowing the principle to take place in your life to help you see the value of his specific prophetic timing for your life. Are you the prophet who feels that time is your enemy when time is a friend and allay that has come to develop you?

Time in a prophet's life builds an infrastructure, which serves as a foundation. It takes time to learn how to fail before you can appreciate how to succeed. This principle is lost in many a prophet's lives. The prophet's zeal robs them of self-understanding time value development in difficult situations of life. Ecclesiastics 3:1 is clear in that there is a season, a special time that is captured and realized as the wheat and tare demonstrate. Time value development teaches two very important concepts the wheat and tares demonstrate.

#1. the prophet must know when to plant and
#2. the prophet must know when to harvest.

The reality of this is that prophets must understand that you can't have a new season while you hold on to what God wants you to let go. Check your life and fill in the blanks on moving from the old season to the new. You can't afford to be unproductive in a new season. It is not the will of God.

Some of us as prophets need to let go of our childish ways and the emotional baggage that has held us back. Can we consider ourselves as we look at our patience? Why are we jumping into things and want no mentoring?

Why are we unwilling to grow but want to assume relevant positions requiring work, that we care not to do? Cross-cultural ministry in the prophet is just that. In 1 Corinthians 13:11, the prophet explores the concept that there is a reality that many prophets are still in the phase of childhood as we explore the mentality of prophetic development.

We must put away childish notions and things that hold us back as prophets and stop delaying the next season of our life. In understanding the differences between prophets, the value of time is a primary factor between a mature and immature prophet. The immature prophet is moved by the crowd, while the mature prophet is moved by a Godly relationship birthed in season.

Go back to Matthew 13 and see that every prophet has a revelation. Isaiah 53:1 speaks to us as prophets about knowing and receiving the Word of God. So with that in mind, receive these five concepts of prophetic timing. Prophets, Matthew 13 reveals the following:

As prophets, our planting good seeds does not alter the planting of bad seeds in our lives. Prophet is simply naive to think that the planting of good will exempt you from the presence of evil. We see this explained in Matthew 13.

1. Just because God allows the wheat does not mean He restricts the tares. Prophet, you are anointed, but that does not mean everyone around you will see or even honor your anointing.

The tares are there because we have to be able to produce in the presence of tares in our lives. Every prophet waiting for something to occur before you go forth, you have missed the very essence of Matthew 13 for the prophet.

The text declares that there will never be a day that you can be free of tares. They will grow together, it is written. God has allowed the wheat to be planted and the tares to grow along with the wheat.

There is a revelation here that as a prophet, you will constantly be faced with challenges of a specific kind until an appointed time. Some challenges will disappear as you ascend to your promoted position.

This is the result of work, and prophets who do not work never reach this position. You will not plant the seed in a day and eat the bread of it that night. Remember that time creates the infrastructure. The infrastructure is what will separate you and even make you feel left, abandoned, but this is the life of Prophetic Development.

2. Where ever there is a place for a great harvest, the enemy will always identify the place with drama. Look in your life and see where there is a great harvest, and you will find some type of chaos.

Weeds are never planted before the wheat; the weeds/tares were planted after the wheat. This is how the wheat and tares grow together.

Prophets, we must stop crying about life, and will you finally realize that all of hell knew that God had a plan for your life and He was going to use you? So yes, hell has been prepared for you for quite some time. Can you see that?

You're not walking in bad luck; you are walking in a blessing. The enemy has a system in place so you would struggle; God allowed you to struggle to take you through the storm to develop you. There is a reality that many things in your life are meant to be, the ups and downs of life. This is how God prepares you for your next assignment.

Satan will always seek to corrupt the environment where God has planted His prophets for development. Satan understands time; that is why he works in the darkness; the scripture says the weeds/tares were planted in the dark while everyone slept.

3. There is a difference between corruption and destruction in a prophet's life. When God's hand is upon the life of a prophet, there is nothing the enemy can do. So here we see God's hand upon His prophet,

and all the enemy can do is corrupt the environment that the prophet lives in.

This is why we see constant drama in prophets' lives. Satan cannot curse what God has blessed. He may be there in your life, but the trials and what people say will not stop you. It did not stop the wheat, and it will not stop you. Look at all your haters and tell them that you are blessed.

The reality of the devil trying to discredit you in multiple ways was evident before you knew who you were. This is how you draw on the power of doing nothing, even as you grow up trusting God. We must learn to stand still as prophets and allow God to do the work within us. This is why we don't grow the tares.

4. There is wisdom in a prophet that learns by waiting. Time is expensive. God said to leave it alone because we were not called to pull the weeds/tares up. Let them grow; in due season, he would do the burning up and the separating.

This is why the prophet needs to learn that the tares assigned to his life, but they have a job to do as well as the prophet. The faith of a prophet is a cult to most believers and clearly to unbelievers. Time is the most expensive seed you will ever plant, and when you realize that, you will start to understand genuine prophetic growth. They that wait upon the Lord shall know.

5. The harvest will never be rushed by the planter and be in His will. God does not and will not rush His prophets to the assignment before you are ready. Prophets, you will kill your destiny if you jump before your harvest. You will destroy something you need because you did not allow the wheat and the tares to grow in your life.

This is what you will need to be prepared mentally for the nations. Understanding cross-cultural ministry with the wheat and tares is an example of knowing not everyone will love you as you come and do the work of God.

When you realize you are going to assignments and places you have never been, realize that your belief system will be tested. Prophet, if you are never tested, then you will never grow, nor will you be trusted by God. The level of your maturity is measured by how you deal with the enemy of your belief. Understand that the enemy of your belief is real.

CHAPTER 8

THE ENEMY OF A PROPHET'S BELIEF

How many of us as prophets realize that it is possible to believe and still walk in unbelief? Prophets, it is entirely possible to see people set free and delivered, and you still listen to the devil about your suspicion. Your journey to the nations will challenge you in this area. The crushing of a prophet will challenge your belief, but you need to realize that you have to learn to deal with your personal unbelief. A prophet who has experience going to the nations will be your best mentor, it matters who you are around.

God cannot use you as a prophet if you have a belief system constantly speaking doubt and disbelief. By now, the chances of you strongly on the battlefield and your belief system have faults. How many of us as prophets believe that? In Mark 9:23-24, Jesus tells the man everything is possible if he believes. He tells Jesus he believes but help his unbelief.

Maybe you are the prophet who will brag about God's power and stress the fact that you do not believe it is strong enough to walk in the divineness of the gift. You know God is able, but will God do it for you is the question you struggle with? Then there are the prophets who can believe for God to open up resources and opportunities and when God does, they do not believe they are supposed to walk into what God has opened. They feel unworthy and retreat to the familiar. You must know where you are at, prophet. You will see this in your cross-culture work.

Are you a prophet who believes but knows you need help with your unbelief? How many of us live daily with contradictions in our lives? How many of us know it, yet we ignore and refuse to address the contradictions?

Many times as a prophet, we are living in the absolute fire of God, and then the next moment, we are drowning in the water of disappear. This will birth the prophetic mood swings and can stir up the bipolar spirit in us. Are you willing to ask God to help your unbelief? Your culture and your prophetic culture has so much to do with what you believe and what you don't believe. Look around you and see what and who you are surrounding yourself with.

Humans think on the level of those we choose to deal with. This same thing goes for the prophetic; you will only think on the level of those you fellowship and receive from. Think about it; your idealism, customs, and traditions are contagious. You are rewarded when you think, express, and communicate a certain way; you are the odd man out when you don't. This is the culture of life itself. This is your culture.

Does everybody want to know what's wrong with you because your belief system has broken away from the pack of mediocrity you may have surrounded yourself with? You have to ask yourself whether you are strong enough to break away from the standard dribble of your life and accept God's will more in your life.

One of the greatest disservices a prophet does to themselves is to know better and refuse to do better. The reality of dumbing down to the environment to fit in is a classic example of a prophet's belief system so faulted that it sways back and forth like the wind.

The ability of prophetically gifted people to self-sabotage themselves is an ever-evolving art. This is why today's prophets and seers must strongly consider schools and gatherings developed to empower them and stretch their thinking to higher levels.

We must also consider how many of us are affected genetically by our belief system. Remember when your relative said it, and it must be the absolute, unquestioned gospel truth? Well, daddy believed it, so it has to be an absolute fact. How many of us today as prophets are defined by a predisposition that defines us as prophets?

Have you ever been greatly affected by something and had no earthly reason why you are affected or feel a certain way about something? How many of you are scared to be alone and do not know why? It is passing and has passed from a previous generation. We can so many times believe them, and then there are times they will not believe us or believe in us as God's prophets. The trauma of what happened in a previous generation to a family member is a reality in your life now and in a later generation.

This trauma was not taught to you. It was passed to you. Generationally you have been affected. The reality is many of today's prophets are struggling to break curses, some are spoken, and many are unspoken, and they are genetically birthed from another generation to today. Read Leviticus 26:40-46 and commit it to your life to break the generational bondage off your life, your children's lives, and their children's lives.

How many of us still eat greens for money and black eye peas for luck on New Year's day? The reality of a generational system of belief being passed down is real. This is a culture and there is no reason to be ashamed if you enjoy it. I remember asking why and was told I was supposed to. Of course, there was no validation of the belief system, except it came from my family, and you better not dispute it; many of you had similar issues. My culture and my ability to be familiar were the deciding factors; they were the enemies I never realized. I, like so many, was comfortable because of the familiarity, but it did little for my growth.

This systemic genetic belief today is still real as you go into the grocery store around the New Year, and one day you will see a pallet of black-eyed peas, which will be placed not far from the greens. Go back in a couple of days, the pallet is gone, and there are no black eye peas or greens. The grocery store manager is happy, and no one questions the belief system, especially if your mom or grandmother is cooking the peas and greens.

Our belief system must be more significant than the car or the new house. The point of knowing that our environment guides our belief system is a reality.

Somehow mentally, we have lowered God's goodness to the number of goods we have. The culture you are affects you, and to realize that you have to be immune to your culture that does not elevate God in your life. Prophets, this is so important because your culture is critically important to who you are and who you are to become. The advent of multiple cultures affects your belief system.

Today, we have the prophetic, church, city, town, and various cultures identified spiritually by the activity of that spirit that prevails there. The reality is that the culture influences the ability to think, and the reasoning is a reality of the common sense of that culture.

Culture will leave a residue on you and your life. The residue will cause you to prescribe to things that, as a prophet, you know are wrong. You must stop speaking, and communicating ideas spreads the residue of failure. The residue of failure is birthed in conflicting dreams and visions.

How many of us have that inner conflict and go to an extreme that births failure as a constant? Inner conflict for a prophet will have a prophet speak what God says to them and then ignore that word for themselves. This is why it is difficult to educate prophets past their belief system. The prophetic will challenge them past their comfort level of belief. Belief in the prophetic ministry will push you to the other side of the belief system you may have been raised in.

How often have we seen prophets come to God, get raised in the anointing, and still fall short of what God wants to do in their life? We are often limited in our beliefs because our beliefs can open us up to controversy, pain, and even contradiction. When this happens, many prophets will regress to the familiar. There is comfort in the familiar, so that is where there is no trauma in our lives. In Luke 5, Jesus tells Simeon to launch out into the deep, despite his working all night for nothing. Simeon's belief system has left him in a place of giving up as he was washing his nets. Jesus pushed him into a new awareness.

Who watching me is settled with nothing? Who is willing to let God through Jesus take you to another level? Who has God gifted in the prophetic, but they have quit on God? Those who have quit have removed themselves spiritually. Who is ready to be disrupted? The question is, who is prepared to be pushed past their comfort level of belief? Can you imagine

Simeon asking Jesus to depart from him because the Words of Jesus had challenged the culture of his life?

The reality of the prophetic is the same for today; just as Simeon was challenged, so are many of today's prophets challenged, and they will run or retreat. The fish catch was the real-life challenge of breaking the wall of unbelief in his life that the culture fed him. Prophet let us realize that our dealing with cultures exposes us to some of the highest levels of demonic activity, so as we learn our culture, we must be ready for what other cultures bring us. The Heil Spirit is a classic example of cultural disrespect.

CHAPTER 9

CULTURE OF THE HEIL SPIRIT

There are four places a prophet must go: Gilgal, the place of faith; Bethel, the place of Decision; Jericho, the place of spiritual warfare and Jordan, where you start to see. All are extraordinary experiences in a prophet's life as they process through their prophetic journey. In the last few chapters, we have focused on developing tools to deal with understanding one's culture as a means to understand and see how other people feel about their culture, the same way you, I, or anyone would.

I cannot stress strongly enough, why becoming respectable to someone's culture is crucial. Look at Jericho in Joshua 6:26. Jericho has fallen, and Joshua prophesied a curse on the man that would rebuild its walls. There was still a man knowing all that who would still rebuild it. This was a prophetic curse released against anyone trying to rebuild what God had destroyed. Like the biblical days, today we have people who do not care. These are the ones who have no regard for anyone's culture except theirs. People who do not fear God and push their beliefs upon you will ostracize you if you do not comply.

In 1 Kings 16:34, Hiel rebuilt the city anyway, dedicating the foundation (structure) and the gates (government) to his two sons. This man knew rebuilding Jericho would bring a curse on him and his family, but he did not care. Can you imagine being brought up in a hate culture and constantly feeding that message? This was the life of Heil.

This spirit of Heil and its sister spirit jealously, we see clearly at work today. People within the prophetic community hate God; some parade themselves as prophets, seers, and even apostles and will do everything they can to rebuild those things God has decreed as wrong. This fits their agenda. This is the Heil Spirit; recognize it and learn how to deal with it.

Today we see that same spirit put one under scrutiny or devalue their ministry, church, or calling. This is funny as we still accept society's new wave of morality. We ask should I tithe, or should I give an offering, in and among the Body of Christ? We ask questions about each other and seek to see who is or is not relevant based on cultural beliefs. We constantly move in the Heil Spirit in our disrespect, and we see nothing wrong with it because we are working only in the context of our culture only.

As prophets included, we find ourselves debating how to be politically correct about things God has cursed and called sin. Whether you agree with me or you do not, there is a total disrespect for others' cultures, not ours, and we constantly fool ourselves about how to fix our issues. To say we need more remnants of Cross-Cultural relationships and ministry is an understatement. This is a lot of real-life work.

We are the Elijah's sent to deal with the spiritual opposition of today's generation. We are here to deal with this generation's Bethelites or Heil spirits. We must clean out our ranks before we can sit back and criticize and judge someone else's model, especially when they have legitimate concerns based on their culture. The core issue is that what may be an issue to me may not be an issue to my brother in Christ of a different culture.

In 1 Kings 16, the term "Bethelite" is associated with Heil. He was the child of the sin of King Jeroboam, and we see that Bethel was invested in sin. Jeroboam acted as a high priest and placed one of his calves on the alter, where he built a temple. The service was to harden the heart of Hiel, his son, as to prepare him to disregard the curse of God. Understand here the hatred and jealousy of God. The point is this was not an issue to Heil. It was an issue to God's people.

What am I saying? This started with Heil's father as he trained his son to hate God. This was the culture he grew up in, and this was how he saw God. This is Ahab's day, so the day's thinking was that the day's climate was one of great wickedness. This must remind you of today.

Heil looks at Ahab and figures if he can do it, so can he. Do what? Ignore God and act as if he could care less. This is unfortunate; we have so many prophets and those within the Body of Christ who exhibit this type of behavior. Funny how some people will do evil because others have done it and do not realize how dangerous it is.

Joshua 6:23 echoes the mending of cultures today in the Body of Christ. A desolate condition, a product of the wickedness of a place, a powerful cursed spirit, the spirit of Heil, a resourceful demonic opponent that many of us never realized, seeks to rebuild and restructure what you have accomplished through prayer. The assignment today is to kill and disrespect a culture, unlike mine. Can we please stop ignoring this and unite the prophetic community of God?

This spirit deals with each of us, and we must recognize that it is real and cares nothing about you or the plan and purpose of God. This spirit knows the Word of God and will not live it. This spirit is cursed and wants to share it by rebelling against God and his prophets. The Heil spirit is an alliance of Jezebel, a direct enemy of prophets and prophetic ministry.

This spirit is in the church today and stands clearly against the oracles of God. This is an enemy of the Prophetic Culture and the Prophetic Community. Notice that we call Jericho the place of warfare; it is the first city that offered outright resistance to the people of God. Heil was a man possessed with the spirit of wickedness. He's not a man of God; he's so defiant. He loses his eldest son when he lays the foundation; he persists in the undertaking and sees his youngest son's death. He paid a significant penalty accordingly.

The reality is he completed the rebuilding of Jericho. Not only did he lay the foundation, but he also set up the gates. Resolution and persistency he showed but the qualities of truth and goodness, the answer is no he is cursed. Does this sound like us today? Prophet, when you ask, "How could a man have been so irresponsible to commit an act that might destroy his family?" Let's look at ourselves; we allow the same things to happen again today. We claim to know God's Word, and we blatantly disobey it, again with full knowledge. We have differences in our cultures, and we call them sins if they are not of our culture.

We totally neglect our duties before God to worship, forgive, surrender ourselves, and give so that we can inherit greater! We can look at Heil, but we would be better off seeing ourselves as we are cursed, and some of us do not know. Heil's experience teaches us that sin has its price. Imagine a man or a woman cursed, and it rests upon you or someone you know.

In Matthew 13:24-30, God wants us to know He is the separator and will determine what kind of corrective action must be taken in one's life who exhibits this type of spirit. So why do we separate ourselves by culture, especially? The habits of one generation can be the addition of another generation. We showed you that with King Jeroboam and his son Heil. Habits are passed just like customs and traditions; we come to accept them in people, allowing them to mature whether they are healthy or unhealthy. The behavior we allow in our lives will become the accepted norm of the next generation.

We are dealing with your inner prophetic man or woman. This is the calling card of the enemy and why he banks on the fact that you will not do the due diligence needed. This means working on yourself to grow mature enough to deal with him. When we sense an enemy, do we ever wonder why they are operating the way they are? Do we look beyond the surface and see why they are hurting? They become our adversary and fuel us to hurt someone else, who we may or may not think will hurt us. It is a test for us to accept differences within each other; yet, the word is clear, love people despite their differences.

Like the spirit of Hiel, let us take the heart of jealously, for example. Jealousy is one of the demonic realm's top four field generals that moves from generation to generation. The jealous spirit becomes an addiction because it was a habit of a previous generation that was never defeated. This spirit is ruthless, and it never will bow to God. Therefore, satan is in the position he is in.

Take these four steps to identify this cursed enemy so you can take steps to stop and defeat this enemy in all our lives. Here are the basic four types of a Hiel of a Jealous Spirit. These are the result of curses in a particular culture. Make no mistake. Identify them and go in prayer.

1. "The Quiet Spirit," know this spirit never has anything positive to acknowledge towards you! This spirit chooses to ignore your blessings and glorify theirs. Understand this spirit feels that your blessings do not count or matter. The spirit has a cousin called, "I'm more important than you, Spirit." These jealous demonic spirits work hand in hand. You must identify this spirit.

2. "The Are You Sure Spirit" asks this question frequently in a similar manner. It will ask but never provide answers or solutions you can use. This would be the cousin spirit of "The If It Were My Spirit." The funny thing is that the 2nd, 3rd, and 4th "Party Information Spirits" are always best friends of "The Are You Sure Spirit." Other cousin spirits of this spirit are "The In Your Face Displeasure Spirit and "The I Want Your Place Spirit."

3. "The I Don't Want You To Know Spirit" doesn't want you to know what they know. This is probably the most sensitive spirit. This spirit wants you to feel that knowing information will diminish them in their mind. "The I Don't Want You To Know Spirit" specializes in this concept. This spirit wants to know your business but not share mine?" You must be crazy!" Don't you find it funny that this spirit always knows a better way but never wants to reveal it openly? This spirit will only release it after the fact!

(In the "like" spirit of "after preaching" and "after prophesying," which are cousin spirits).

4. "The I Release Myself Spirit" works when a person(s) distance themselves from you or your spirit. They lack the character to tell you why directly but find alternative reasons for the unexplained release. You must understand that the distance is not in what you are doing but in the "perceived perception" of what they see. Perception is everything when you allow limits in your life. Understand this, "They Will NOT," and You Will, so they can't function where "They Will NOT." This is why the anointed release is such a mystery to them.

They would rather not physically see your success so they can speculate freely on your perceived unworthiness of the anointing. (Maybe you will now understand why sometimes your support is so limited). Why do we forget James 1:5? If any lacks wisdom (the principle of anointing), let him ask? Does your enemy ask God for your gift, or does your enemy ask God to remove you?

Cain did not ask God to show him "why" before he killed Abel. If your enemy is speaking to God about you, rest assured God is not listening to a request that will go against His Word. The curse of your enemy is your opportunity to make a mark upon someone's life that will manifest in due season.

We do not always see the results of your struggle, but God does, and He will judge you and elevate you in your due season. "Thou prepareth a table before me in the presence of my enemies, thou anointeth my head with oil; indeed goodness and mercy shall follow me all the days of my life."

I can tell you that this chapter has wrapped itself up in the cultural bias of what we may refer to as a form of racism that is well trained to function in the Body of Christ. All this is because we are from different cultures; the answer is yes, and how much do we give of ourselves to different cultures?

SO I AM A PROPHET IN MY FEELINGS?

Can you imagine someone speaking to you, someone of influence, someone who may be well known, and they come to you and speak something upon your life? The announcement changes your life, or it even may disturb your life. How do you handle it? Your feelings about what you heard are making you feel strange.

Yes, those are only a few of the possible emotions we shall see in the Body of Christ. We learn as prophets how to process our feelings and how to deal with the principles of God that ultimately change our lives. A young man named Jeremiah is a classic example. As we all know, he is called to be a prophet to the nations; we see him hear the Words of God in his life. Jeremiah 1:4-5.

He says the Word of the Lord came saying, I knew thee, and I ordained thee a prophet unto the nations. Prophet, like Jeremiah, that is mind-blowing, hearing those words for the first time, and imagine how you would respond. Yet today, how do we respond to messages from God's servants who communicate the following because their culture is different? Things like:

1. My Culture interprets it this way, and any other way is wrong.

2. Our cultural leaders are equipped to lead us, but other cultural leaders are not.

3. Prophets of my culture are to be respected, while we ignore those of other cultures.

4. A prophetic voice is good enough to minister to people of their culture but never given the opportunity to minister to those of different cultures because there is an unspoken perception about that person because of their culture.

5. The culture of a prophet is criticized and judged, and the very perception blocks that prophet from building and having covenant relationships with other prophets who come out of different cultures.

6. Constant social issues of the day are displayed and reflect on the culture of a prophet, and that prophet struggles to see a positive role model of other cultures supporting his culture in deeds and action.

7.The counter-culture of a prophet's culture forces the prophet to struggle within their own culture. The lack of prophetic development programs, lack of personalized development, and overall lack of unity in the prophetic community have forced difficult paths for some prophets who originate from various cultures.

8. Cultural stress from economic, generational, and cultural divisions created by governmental and historical issues have created cultural division within the prophetic community on how we define who is and who is not a prophet.

9. Religious bias toward the Prophet and Apostle's foundational gifts, including the seer and watchman gifts, has created great division culturally.

10. Cultural courage to be different in our prophetic gifts has not been encouraged, much less among cultures. The is so much arrogance, jealousy, and lack of respect within today's prophetic culture groups that our relationships are strained, nonexistent, and lacking to build effective cross-culture bridges that we need to duplicate the activity of prophetic leaders for Christ.

There are so many other reasons that could be added to this list. We struggle to find basic human dignity within the culture of the Body of Christ. Understand now that God has some real people, and yet we must know that we will deal with all who He chooses for us and when. So look and see a prophet in their feelings. Some will say that you missed what God had for you because of feeling a certain way.

That's an issue because if you have not been exposed, you cannot relate. The failure to have exposure to the issues of another prophet's culture, you are not qualified to speak and judge your prophetic peer.

The things we can do like prayer, encouragement, and honest heart-to-heart dialogue on issues of our cultures that are uncomfortable are priceless in this day and time.

Then there are so many prophets and seers who have depended on their gifting and not allowed God the Word of God to penetrate our mentality. We are not submitted to the Word unless we can see and discern how it will benefit us. We feel we can do that, and others should not. The Word of God moves past cultures and their walls of specific identity.

What seems so hard for us is when we do not accept, we do not receive what God is saying, and our feelings become the hidden enemy in our life; we never identify. While this soliloquy is for Prophets and Seers, there is an equitable distribution of this for other 5-Fold Ministry gifts.

Jeremiah 1:5 takes on a new significance. As we look again, God speaks to Jeremiah. Jeremiah is alerted to the fact that God knew him before he entered time itself. The spoken Word is relevant here that every prophet of God should acknowledge.

This is about relationship, a relationship with God that allows us to believe Him and respect someone else's beliefs and, most of all, their culture. Paul said he became what he needed to become to reach people for Christ.

What has happened to seeking God for what we cannot process or understand? Our relationship with him should stabilize our trust even at this point in our lives. So many times, we allow our feelings to block or tarnish the blessing of God.

Simply put, we do not understand why we are different; why are you saying this to me? We ask ourselves, "God, you say you love me, but you set me apart and send people in my life who say they love you but live life in a different way."

Have you ever talked to yourself and said, "You did this, God, by that one word you spoke or the one You sent someone to speak it?" You said it, but I did not see it or understand it. Little did I realize that was where and what I needed to grow.

Only if Jeremiah were here today, we would appreciate him so much differently. Look at his life; his servitude measures his greatness to God as an outsider who was a reflection of the life he lived.

Judges 6 speaks loud to each of our lives as prophets, and it does not matter what culture we are in or not in. We are like Gideon, who threshed wheat by the winepress to hide it from the Midianites. The angel of God appeared unto him and said unto him, "The Lord is with thee, thou mighty man of velour." Gideon was out of his comfort zone. He was not ready, not acceptable of this word spoken by the angel of God upon his life.

Gideon is speaking from his heart. This is his reality. This is all he knows. Now the Word of God comes to him and changes, challenges him, and he is distressed. He does not see it; his feelings are not in agreement with it, and he is quite articulate as he speaks to the angel that the Lord has forsaken his people. His small tribe is not able to withstand the Midianites.

Have you ever been there before? God has spoken, and the word upon you disagrees with everything your current situation dictates. In your mind, you know it is God, but you do not want to accept it or even consider it. Gideon is having a prophetic growth moment, like many of us have, and it is uncomfortable. The reality of chaos in his life is more significant than what he hears or receives.

Have you been there? God is using your enemies to teach you something you need to know and employ in your life. This is why this book is important to me and maybe only a handful of others.

Our zeal to grow had identified some of the most unspoken and uncomfortable things in the Body of Christ. Like Gideon, what he feared was the very thing God would change. My prayer for the Body of Christ and the prophetic community is that we grow from our most uncomfortable issues in this generation.

Again, prophet, understand that God uses your enemies to bring you into your destiny. Gideon is hiding his harvest in the wine press from the Midianites, so he is threshing his harvest. Should his enemies find out about his harvest, they will take it. They hate Gideon and his people. Gideon is trying to hide what he is blessed with. There is more to this as Gideon is in the wine press.

Have you ever asked why your family is still drowning in drama? Why is my child not doing right? Why is my spouse doing this or that? Why do the people say this or that about me and know absolutely nothing about me?

The transition of moving from your feelings is a process that many repeatedly go through. Transition is a process that brings every feeling and every emotion to the forefront.

Can you understand why your doubt shows up, why your bad feelings show up as you are placed somewhere that in your eyesight is unstable, and it will need more than a word to correct this situation? The reality is that an unstable environment activates your core strength. Welcome to the Prophetic Culture.

The threshing floor for Gideon is an unstable environment. This is why we see him appear to be tripping. He does not see God in his situation. Gideon, just like us, is asking why God does not do it the way he imagines he should do things. God is shaking away the things off of Gideon that are needed to help him make sense of his life.

Being called to the prophetic is no small chore. Prophet, have you ever been in a place where it seemed like the walls were closing in upon you, and someone spoke something that is totally foreign to the situation you are dealing with? The word has no relevance, and your feelings are a mess. This is a culture that takes time to digest for sure.

The process to discover your prophetic identity is a disruptive process. The issue of my feelings is relevant as my feelings move me away from my destiny. We always feel that our feelings should support who we are, but that clearly is not the case with our lives. Too many of us want to blame, hate and belittle who we have become.

We now are now spoken to based on who we are designed to be versus the feelings we are dealing with of our current status. Can you see why we just cannot seem to get it? Our feelings are blocking us from our destiny.

The angel spoke to Gideon based on who he was to become; the prophetic word spoken into your life was based on who you were to be for God. You must choose whether you will become what you are called to, or will you rely on your feelings and be comfortable with what you know about yourself.

God will send someone to your life to tell you who you are and who you are to become. Prophets, it is possible not to know who you will become initially. Your feelings and emotions come and go as they blend in with the process of being familiar; it is always easier.

The reality is that your feelings do not validate your reality. Gifted people, gifted prophets, and seers who strive forward and develop the mentality do not allow their feelings to disrespect the reality of where God has them in life. Notice they still have feelings, yet they know who they are, despite their feelings.

Prophets, you must understand that your feelings cannot always be trusted; they must be surrendered to God, or make no mistake, they will betray you. Your feelings will position you in places that expose you as not having this or not having that, and you actually have it.

This is why culture is dangerous because it will parade in your life as something super special. While it is, it is not special enough to override who God has called you to be, despite what one culture says about another culture.

You and I want to depend on the untrained, unstable, and unmentored feelings that make quick judgments on our limited scope of our culture, knowledge, and history.

Prophet, realize that your feelings are about what has happened and not what is about to happen. Always remember that prophet. God is calling you to where you have not been and calling you to what you have not done. Move your feelings out of the way because the word for your life is an announcement that is supposed to shake you, thresh you, and separate you.

ABOUT THE AUTHOR

Apostle Ken Cox started serving God in 1994 after a series of unforeseen life failures. Out of the military and seemly starting life over again, by 2000, Apostle Cox had found his life calling as a Prophet. The challenge of learning and understanding presented a new frontier. Apostle Cox dove into the process and has now emerged as a well-traveled prophet who serves the Body of Christ as an Apostle.

Apostle Cox, along with his wife, Prophetess Sabina Cox are the leaders of Where Eagles Fly Fellowship Inc., a fellowship of prophets and apostle across the USA and beyond who are dedicated and focused on establishing the prophetic gift back into society as they raise up prophets around the country and abroad.

Apostle Cox and Prophetess Cox are available for Revivals, Conferences and Meetings. They have been featured in meetings and sought-after to teach and instruct the prophetic for ministries seeking to learn more about the gift. Apostle and Prophetess Cox have 3 children and 4 grandkids as of this writing and currently reside in Durham, NC. Contact them through the Where Eagles Fly office at 919-695-3375 or 919-213-1328 or at www.whereeaglesfly.us.

INDEX

H

I

M

N

T

Z